A hungry billy goat ate my coat

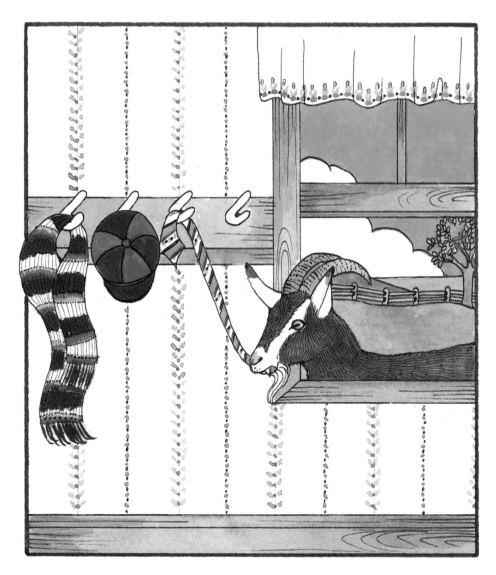

A ROOKIE READER®

THE HUNGRY BILLY GOAT

By Rita Milios

Illustrations by Ching

Prepared under the direction of Robert Hillerich, Ph.D.

 CHILDRENS PRESS®
CHICAGO

Library of Congress Cataloging-in-Publication Data

Milios, Rita.
  The hungry billy goat.

  (A Rookie reader)
  Summary: After a billy goat eats all of his clothes, a
little boy decides to stay far away from goats in the
future.
  [1. Goats—Fiction. 2. Stories in rhyme.]
I. Ching, ill. II. Title. III. Series.
PZ8.3.M59Hu   1989   [E]   89-673
ISBN 0-516-02090-0

and then he ate my tie.

I said, "Don't do that."

7

But he ate my hat,

and then he ate my scarf.

He ate on and on.
He ate the lawn,

and then he ate my shoe.

It got stuck in his throat
so I gave him some soap.

But when he felt better,
he ate my sweater,

and then he ate my shirt.

What he ate next
I can only guess,
for I was not there.

I had no wish
to be his favorite dish,

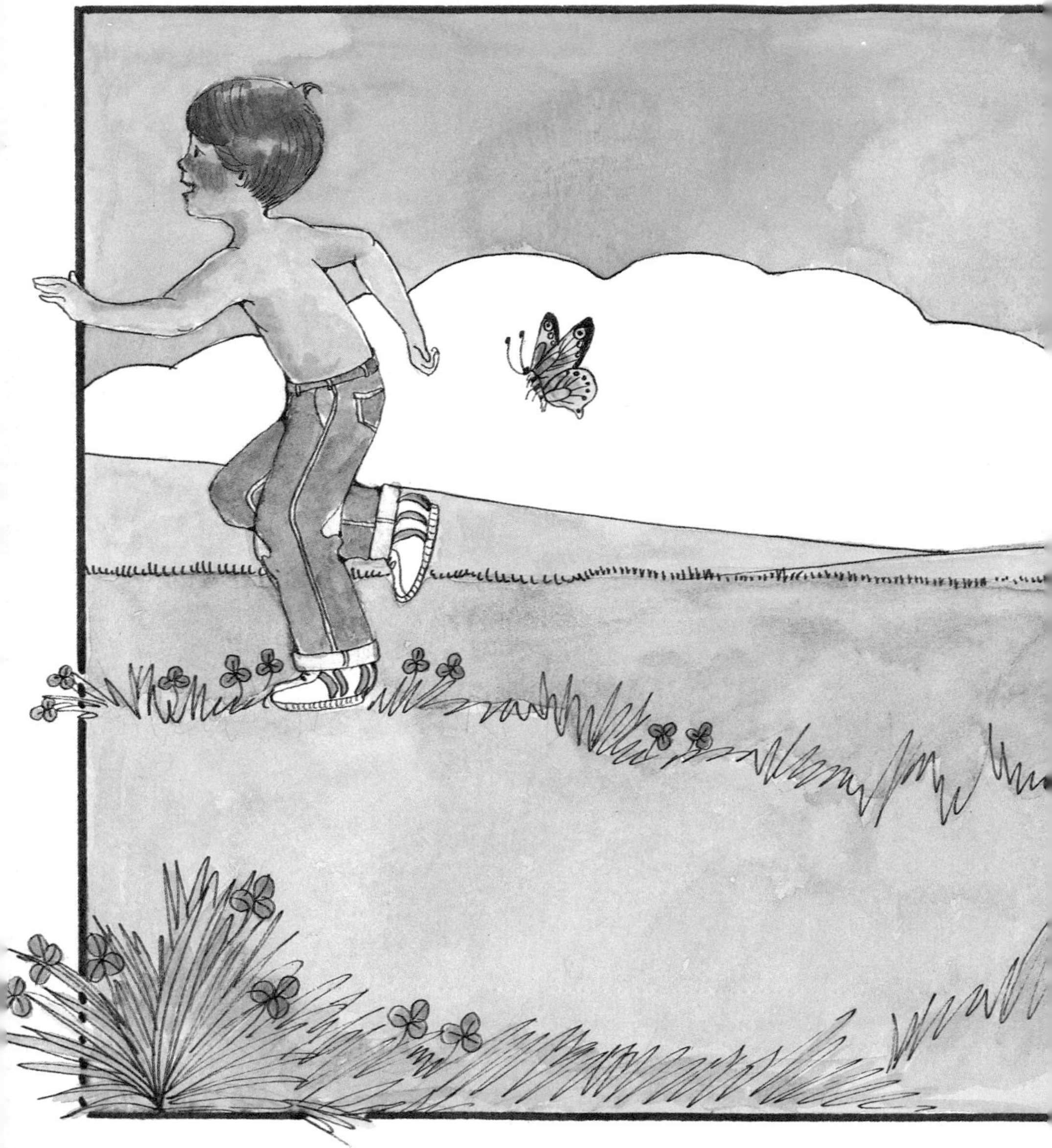

so I ran far, far away.

And to this very day
I stay far away
from hungry billy goats.

WORD LIST

a	felt	it	stay
and	for	lawn	stuck
ate	from	my	sweater
away	gave	next	that
be	goat	no	the
better	goats	not	then
billy	got	on	there
but	guess	only	this
can	had	ran	throat
coat	hat	said	tie
day	he	scarf	to
dish	him	shirt	very
do	his	shoe	was
don't	hungry	so	what
far	I	soap	when
favorite	in	some	wish

About the Author

Rita Milios lives in Toledo, Ohio with her husband and two grade-school children. She is a free-lance writer and instructor in the Continuing Education department at Toldeo University. She has published numerous articles in magazines including *McCall's*, *Lady's Circle*, and *The Writer*. She is currently working on her first adult book. Mrs. Milios is the author of *Sleeping and Dreaming* in the New True Book series and *I Am* and *Bears, Bears Everywhere* in the Rookie Reader series.

About the Artist

Mary "Ching" Walters has twenty-three years of experience as a free-lance artist with primary concentration in the area of postage stamp design, wildlife paintings and illustrations for many greeting card companies. She has illustrated several children's books. Originally from Tennessee, "Ching" currently lives in St. Louis, Mo. with her husband Bob, a TWA pilot, and their dog "Sandy."

12-13-03

B. 7

1/900